Small bronze knife pendant decorated with a fisherman
hauling in a fish by rope; found by Bingham in Serpent Rock area

Machu Picchu

REVEALED

Picchu

A Picture Book

Ruth M. Wright

JOHNSON BOOKS
BOULDER

OVERVIEW

Machu Picchu, a royal estate of Inca Emperor Pachacuti, was built in the Andes in one of the most spectacular settings in South America. It began around 1450 A.D. and ceased functioning about ninety years later, after the Spanish Conquistadors destroyed the Inca Empire.

Machu Picchu is roughly 13 degrees south of the equator and situated on a narrow ridge between the Huayna Picchu and Machu Picchu mountains, at about 8,000 feet in elevation. The ridge drops off steeply on both sides to the Urubamba River 1,500 feet below. The river, a headwater stream of the Amazon River that the Inca considered sacred, nearly encircles Machu Picchu, adding to the site's religious significance.

No one who has watched the early rays of the sun slip down Huayna Picchu Mountain, or the mist rise from the Urubamba River to envelop the ancient buildings, can remain untouched by the mystical beauty of Machu Picchu. Here all the elements of Inca cosmology came together in one place—the mountains, the holy Urubamba River, melted snows from Mt. Salcantay, the heavens and the Pleiades, and the Sun God Inti, who blessed this place with warm temperatures, creating a respite from the winter weather of Cusco. Natural phenomena are well represented here— clouds, mist rising up from the river, wind and rain, sunshine, stars, rainbows, and thunder are all very much part of the environment. Machu Picchu is ringed by *apus*, the mountain gods of the high Andes, with their snow-covered peaks and glaciers. And it also has one very necessary and practical ingredient—pure spring water from Machu Picchu Mountain.

To create his royal retreat, Pachacuti assembled the best talent—engineers, planners, designers, stonecutters, craftsmen, and artisans from all over the empire. With his retinue of priests, noblemen, and families, he came here to renew his spirits, to

hunt the bounty of nature, and above all, to pray to the gods to bless the people and grant them successful harvests. Pachacuti would be pleased to know that his landscape and architectural gem was recently designated one of the "new" seven wonders of the world (2007).

Machu Picchu's remote location saved it from destruction when the Inca empire collapsed. The site was simply abandoned, to be rediscovered by Yale professor and explorer Hiram Bingham in 1911. His photos and stories in *National Geographic* magazine astounded the world.

With this pictorial essay I would like to share with you the wonderful accomplishments of the Inca represented at this challenging site. They were creative in embellishing the beauty of nature and blending their structures with the environment. They were masters of stonework, incorporating the sight and sound of flowing water while combining their cosmology with the practical necessities of a living community.

—R.W.

WIÑAY WAYNA TO MAIN GATE

The Inca built a paved stone trail all the way from Cusco, the Inca capital, to Machu Picchu, with *tambos* (inns) along the way. The last inn before Machu Picchu was at Wiñay Wayna. The following morning travelers would reach Intipunku (Gate of the Sun), then proceed down to the Guardhouse and through the Main Gate.

Inca engineers demonstrated that they knew how to combine beauty with practicality when they designed the exquisite fountains at Wiñay Wayna and channeled water from a nearby river to flow through them for the tambo *visitors.*

Above: The paved Inca Trail leading up to the last ridge before Machu Picchu at Intipunku, Gate of the Sun.
Right: The Inca Trail angles in from the left, and the small Guardhouse controls in-coming visitors and overlooks all of the royal estate.

Left: Modern-day chaskqui *(messengers or porters) rest at Intipunku before their final dash down to the Main Gate.*

Above: A chaskqui *above the security station at the junction of two trails.*

Left: The security station had good control over the llama "pack trains" that would bring supplies to the royal retreat, and had a fine view to Machu Picchu from its platform.
Above: It also had a huaca *(carved rock shrine).*

Left: The Guardhouse is built on a bluff, with aesthetic terraces curving along natural contours.
Above: The Guardhouse is a wayrona *structure—a three-sided building with one side open. "Flying steps" were used to go from one terrace to another.*

Above: Watching the sunrise from the Guardhouse is a sight never to be forgotten. The sun slips down the face of Huayna Picchu Mountain to touch the sacred center with its magic. Right: As the sun rises, more and more of Machu Picchu is revealed. Its intriguing Western Sector and the equally inviting Eastern Sector come into view, separated by the green swath of the Main Plaza.

Above: Here the Main Gate frames the holy Huayna Picchu Mountain, a fitting introduction to the architectural gem beyond. This is the front door, where the Inca ruler and his retinue would have arrived with great pomp. The storehouses on the right would have been filled with the produce of a successful empire. Right: The inside of the gate shows how it could have been closed from intruders: the built-in stone ring above the gate and the barholds on either side probably were used to bar the entrance.

TEMPLE OF THE SUN

The sacred center was the inspiration for several magnificent temples where the Inca and priests conducted ceremonies for their gods. In a prime location adjacent to the Royal Residence, the Temple of the Sun was dedicated to Inti, the sun god. The temple holds the first of a series of fountains, bringing precious pristine water from a spring on Machu Picchu Mountain.

Opposite: The Temple of the Sun (bottom left), with its semicircular wall, is in a prominent and central location.
Right: The wall protects and honors the huge sacred rock on which the temple is built. A thatch-roofed wayrona and the Royal Residence lie beyond.

Left: At sunrise on the June solstice the sunlight coming through the window is bisected by the ledge. Above: Some have speculated that the ledge cut in the rock, together with the strategically placed eastern window, created a solar observatory.

Above: This view explains why the Spanish called it the "Torreon," or tower. The stairway in the foreground was cut from a single piece of granite—a showpiece of Inca stone shaping. Right: Underneath the same rock that the Temple of the Sun is built on is a natural cave, known as the Royal Tomb because it is believed that mummies of the Inca or priests were placed here for worship.

The abstract sculpture at the entrance could signify mountains.

The sculpture as seen from the inside. Mt. Yanantin is in the far distance.

Opposite: The most beautiful double-jamb doorway in Machu Picchu leads into the holy complex. A double-jamb doorway signified a special place beyond. Left: On the inside are the barholds and ring above, showing that the doorway could be closed, at least symbolically, with a rope or bar. All of the doorways, windows, and niches had a trapezoidal shape—both for stability and beauty. This area has not been reconstructed—the Inca built for the ages.

Above: On the north side is the Enigmatic Window, so named because of its unusual shape and the holes in the stones. These were likely used to attach sacred objects, perhaps made of gold. The Guardhouse dominates the view.

Left: From inside the wayrona, *we share the same view that the Inca priests had: Putucusi Mountain on the right and the mountains of the Urubamba Valley receding into the distance.*

Above: An adjacent carved rock would have been used for ceremonial purposes at the wayrona, *perhaps honoring the water flowing through the temple complex.*

SACRED PLAZA

The Sacred Plaza is located below and on the way to the Intiwatana Pyramid. Two of Machu Picchu's most important temples are on the Sacred Plaza. The plaza construction was a work in process, probably halted when the empire fell to the Spaniards. The royals would never come here again.

Above: The view to the west is awe inspiring.
Right: The Principal Temple lies on the north side.
It has a huge altar-like stone along the back wall.

Right: The Temple of the Three Windows is three-sided and opens to the Sacred Plaza. It has the largest windows in Machu Picchu, overlooking the Main Plaza, which is below. Originally there were five windows—the ones on the right and the left were closed to form niches. This temple, made of gigantic polygonal (many sided) stones, was never finished.

Above: Of particular interest is the settlement of the right wall of the Principle Temple, which happened during Inca times and is probably the reason construction was halted on that particular building. In this rare failure of Inca construction, inadequate foundation work permitted the right wall to settle, pulling the stones of the back wall to the right without completely displacing them.

Left: From a window in the Eastern Sector the temple is impressive and shows that here the Inca built the proper foundations with several terraces adequately supporting the heavy stones. Broken keros *(ceramic drinking cups) were found on the terraces, indicating ritualistic breaking for ceremonies in the temple. Above: Views through the windows looking east.*

Left and right: Closeup views through the windows show llamas peacefully grazing in front of the Artisans' Wall and tourists heading up the grand staircase.

INTIWATANA

The morning sun highlights the natural Intiwatana Pyramid. Carved by Inca stonecutters from the peak itself, the Intiwatana Stone is not a sundial, but a sculptural expression of the sacred majesty of this high point in Machu Picchu. With a breathtaking 360-degree view of the mountains and valleys, all of Machu Picchu unfolds beneath you. There is no doubt that important religious ceremonies were performed here.

Opposite: Just north of the Sacred Plaza, a grand staircase of matching granite steps leads to the top of the Intiwatana Pyramid. The Intiwatana Stone can be seen as a small protrusion just beyond the buildings.
Right: Sometimes called the "Hitching Post of the Sun," one can imagine the sun being ritually tied to the rock so when it sets in the west it will reappear in the east.

Left: The carved Intiwatana replicates the holy mountain Huayna Picchu in an abstract way.
Above: Another view, with Machu Picchu Mountain in the background.

Left: Also at the top of the Intiwatana Pyramid are stones carved to replicate the peaks of Mount Yanantin (on the left) and the rounded Putucusi (on the right). Perhaps such stones were meant to communicate with the apus, *the holy mountains.*

Above: Evening is a time for quiet reflection. The beautiful terraces are designed to protect the steep slopes of the pyramid.

Left: Looking toward the Eastern Sector, a storm has come and gone, creating a dramatic contrast with the dark mountains silhouetted beyond.
Above: The Intiwatana Pyramid now becomes a silhouette against the clouds.

EASTERN SECTOR

Like most Inca communities, Machu Picchu is divided into higher and lower sectors—not necessarily determined by geography, but by status, with a plaza between the two. The higher sector here is the Western Sector, with its Temple of the Sun, Sacred Plaza, Intiwatana, and Royal Residence. The Eastern Sector, however, is not to be outdone. Of special note are several sites: the Sacred Rock, the Unfinished Temple and the inimitable Temple of the Condor. Some of the general views of the Eastern Sector are magnificent and very photogenic.

A long granite staircase leads down to the Artisans' Wall. Mount Yanantin peeks over the clouds, and the rounded Putucusi looms in the center—both are on the other side of the Urubamba River.

Above: The grand staircase leads up to a residential area that was for visiting nobility.
Right: A different perspective shows the outer wall of the Temple of the Condor
on the right and Huayna Picchu on the left.

Above: Sunset bathes the outer wall of the Temple of the Condor and the huge wayrona *in a golden hue.*
Right: Early morning sun highlights the geometric harmony of Inca design with its environment.

Left: The strong vertical relief of Machu Picchu was mastered by the Inca architects with granite stairways and terrace walls incorporated with natural stone outcrops.

Above: A landscape masterpiece—from the flowers in the foreground, out across the Main Plaza, to the pointed buildings of the Eastern Sector, with the mountains receding into the pale blue distance.

SACRED ROCK

The Sacred Rock area is a small U-shaped shrine, with a rock as its centerpiece, and is flanked by two *wayronas*, creating a private space. Unlike elsewhere in Machu Picchu, where the natural formations were embellished, this rock was brought to the site and placed on a stone pedestal. The rock itself is about 25 feet long, 10 feet high, and 2 feet thick. This shrine would have been used for smaller ceremonies. Interestingly, it is still so used by the Quechua Indians. Just beyond the Sacred Rock, the trail to Huayna Picchu begins.

The Sacred Rock complex lies to the east (right) of the Intiwatana Pyramid, with the two thatch-roofed wayronas. *To its left in the background is Uña Picchu, which also has abundant terraces.*

Opposite: The thatched roof of the wayrona *has been rebuilt. Alpaca graze in the foreground.*

Above: The Sacred Rock mimics the peak of Mount Yanantin beyond. This shrine provides a mystical setting for ceremonies that continue to this day.

Left: A bouquet of lilies has been placed against the rock, probably as an offering.

UNFINISHED TEMPLE

Adjacent to the Sacred Rock are granite pinnacles at the top of a large mound. Massive stones were used to create tight-fitting terrace walls. This unfinished temple still has a ramp for moving stones from one level to the next, demonstrating Inca construction techniques. It would have been one of Machu Picchu's most impressive temples.

The Inca utilized hammerstones to shape the rocks used in constructing walls and buildings. These hammerstones were recovered from our 2001 excavations at the Unfinished Temple.

TEMPLE OF THE CONDOR

The Temple of the Condor is the most theatrical of the temples, using natural rock features to the ultimate. The focal point is a stylized flat condor rock, with eyes, beak, and ruff. Behind it are the "wings," creating an image of a condor swooping down to catch its prey. The condor is the largest South American bird, with a wingspan of up to eight feet. It is still revered as a symbol of power and majesty today. The temple is complex, with many levels and subterranean caves.

The Temple of the Condor from above. The triangular in situ *rock is carved in the shape of a condor. Additional white rocks form the "ruff," a characteristic of condors. The natural rocks behind it form huge outspread "wings."*

One of the condor "wings," with Inca stonework on top to heighten the impression of a wing in flight.

Left: While the "wings" are natural formations, they have been embellished by Inca stonemasons, showing the intentional design. One can imagine the creativity of the Inca architect who first saw the possibilities of this unique site.

Top: A closer view of the condor rock's three stones: one forming the body and head, with carved eyes and beak, and two stones forming the ruff.
Above: With just a few cuts, a stone becomes the head of a condor.

Above: The Andean condor, South America's largest bird. (Courtesy National Geographic *magazine.)*
Right: Fountain sixteen is very private in that it is accessible only from the Temple of the Condor.

HUAYNA PICCHU

Huayna Picchu is not just a magnificent backdrop for Machu Picchu, but also an integral part of the sacred center. Huayna Picchu was a holy mountain, to be revered and used for religious ceremonies. It was terraced to prevent erosion and allow for farming of specialty crops such as maté, a South American tea. Trails and granite stairways were built so the Inca and priests could easily access the top, with a 360-degree view to all the high *apus* of the Andes. On the way to the summit there was a security observation post, a viewing platform, and even a tunnel.

Right: Huayna Picchu towers over the buildings in the Eastern Sector. The building perched on the left near the top of the mountain has been reconstructed. Opposite: The many steep terraces built on the rocky ridges provide stability. The sacred center is far below (upper left), as is the Urubamba River (lower right).

Left: The long stairway goes straight up to the viewing platform beyond.
Above: Terraces drop off precipitously to the ridge below.

*Above: One summit route goes through
a tunnel.*
*Right: The terraces are narrow and tall
to hold the steep slope in place.*

*A curved stairway
leads down to a
remote terrace.*

Above: Stairways abound near the summit of Huayna Picchu.
Right: A security lookout station with important pointed granite rocks
and a long view over to the Intiwatana Pyramid.

Above: An usnu-*type structure overlooks all of Machu Picchu. An* usnu *was usually a small three-tiered platform used throughout the empire in various ways—as an altar, throne, place of prayer, or symbol of power and government.*
Right: Remote and hidden stairways and terraces add to the mystery of Huayna Picchu. The two-story grain storehouse had views to Llactapata, another Inca site, across the valley to the west.

TEMPLE OF
THE MOON

O n the back side of Huayna Picchu is a
temple not often visited due to its re-
moteness. It is accessed in one of two ways: via
a trail that goes around Huayna Picchu Mountain to the north side, or up and over Huayna
Picchu with a steep trail descending on the
north side. It was never mentioned by Hiram
Bingham, and its name was chosen simply as a
counterpart to the Temple of the Sun in the
1930s. There is no indication that the moon was
worshiped here. The temple is tucked under a
large overhang, or cave, and the niches were cut
into the rock itself. There are also various structures in the complex, including a very tall dou-
ble-jam doorway.

*This was an appropriate site for a temple: a
cave on the slope of a holy mountain. Caves, like
springs, were thought to be entrances for the gods.*

Left: Fine stonework and triple-jamb frames for the niches show that this was an important site.

Above: The tallest double-jamb doorway in Machu Picchu, with the jambs on the down-slope side. This may indicate that this temple was approached from the Urubamba River via a trail through the lower forest; however, it could also be visited from Machu Picchu itself.

WATER

When planning a new community, clean drinking water is an absolute necessity. The Inca found such a source in the forest on the flank of Machu Picchu Mountain, just a half mile from the proposed center. It was a spring, the result of fractures in the rock and the almost 80 inches of rainfall each year. The engineers captured the water and brought it to the center in a creatively designed canal, on its own terrace and at just the right grade. From there it flowed freely down through sixteen fountains for ceremonial purposes and as a domestic water supply for the inhabitants, who would fill their *aryballos* (pottery bottles).

Right: The water flows out of the forest past a storehouse.
Far right: From the storehouse the water flows on its own terrace into the sacred center.

Above: The first of the sixteen fountains, adjacent to the royal residence, gave the emperor the best quality water. (Tests have shown the water, which still flows from the spring, to be of exceptional quality.) Each fountain is different but basically of the same design: a spout, a receiving basin, niches in the privacy walls, an outlet, and a channel to the next fountain. Right: At the Temple of the Sun the water flows through the Sacred Fountain and along the Stairway of the Fountains in an imaginative and creative manner. The builders obviously used the sight and sound of running water to enhance the religious site. Water was revered as life giving and sustaining, and springs were particularly sacred.

The fountains are really drop structures made of cut granite stones.

Left: The water flows continuously and uninterrupted from one fountain to the next, until the final fountain discharges the water into the main drain.

Top: The spout was designed to jet the water so that an aryballo *(pottery bottle) could be filled and carried to the living quarters.*

Above: An Inca aryballo, *famous for its high-quality production and used throughout the empire.*

LONG LOST TRAIL ON THE EAST FLANK OF MACHU PICCHU

It was long suspected that the fabled Inca Trail continued beyond Machu Picchu and down to the Urubamba River. In 1996 the Wright Paleological Institute team decided to explore that possibility. Over the next three years field trips to the East Flank resulted in astonishing discoveries—not only of the trail, with granite stairs nine feet wide, but also of terraces, and most exciting, fountains as beautiful as the ones along the Stairway of the Fountains. The following pictures record these discoveries. (The trail is not open to the public due to its steep slopes and important wildlife habitat for the rare and endangered Spectacled Bear.)

Opposite: Looking down to the river from Machu Picchu to develop a strategy for exploration. Right: To access the trail from below, a river crossing was first used. But with a rising flow and downstream cataracts, it proved too dangerous.

Left: A safer route involved heading around a bluff to access the likely location of the trail.
Above: Macheteros *(men wielding machetes) clearing dense forest.*

Left: Uncovering stairways and terraces on the steep slope above the Urubamba River.
Above: Ken Wright records the early discovery of ceremonial fountains.

Above: Additional work clearing the two most extraor-
dinary fountains.
Right: The magnificent stairways, trail, terraces, and
retaining wall long covered by forest.

Above: After clearing farther down the slope, the team discovers a retain-
ing wall built on top of natural rock and a stairway cut from in situ *rock.*
Right: The cleared areas reveals extensive terraces, trails, and fountains; the
view is from Huayna Picchu.

Above: Most exciting is the discovery of the fountains. It is a thrill when the debris and dirt are cleaned away—like magic the water starts flowing again after 500 years, pristine enough to drink.
Right: The author points to the remarkable design of the inlet channel that causes the spring water to jet over the wall.

Opposite: A year later, softened by the new greenery that had grown around it, the fountain was still flowing!
Left: One of the macheteros *who had uncovered the fountain was so moved that he took a piece of his bread and prayed to the* apus *(mountain gods) and* Pacha Mama *(Earth Goddess) to keep the waters flowing forever, and buried his offering in the ground below the fountain.*

QUECHUA INDIANS

The Quechua Indians of the Andes are descendants of the Inca. Quechua was the language of the Inca and was spoken widely, especially throughout the northern part of the empire. The Quechua are hardworking, friendly, magnanimous people who delight in their families and traditions. On market day in Pisac, for example, the various groups dress in their colorful village garb to distinguish themselves from others. They also love celebrations, dancing, and religious ceremonies. Some of these ceremonies are "native" and are meshed with Christianity, both condoned and accepted by the Catholic Church. Here is a photographic sampling of their life and world, from bathing a baby in the courtyard, to markets with fruits and vegetables of infinite variety, to mothers carrying their little ones in shawls, to dancers with exotic costumes—not for tourists, but for their own pleasure and entertainment.

LLAMAS

The resident llamas at Machu Picchu are a friendly group. They wander freely, quietly munch the grasses, hop from one terrace to another, and have no difficulty going up the granite stairs. Some have tiny bells tied to their ears and will let you scratch them. The Inca did not have the wheel, probably because the terrain, both steep and rocky, was not well suited to wheeled vehicles. Instead they had the llama, a versatile, gentle creature that requires very little care, is intelligent and easily trained. They are able to pack about 100 pounds, their fur produces very soft fiber for weaving, and ultimately are meat on the hoof. Llamas are camelids, a family of large herbivores, which in South America includes alpaca and vicuña.

Right: Llamas doing what they do best—keeping the grass mowed.
Opposite: Looking over its domain at the grand staircase in the Eastern Sector.

Right: At rest in the Main Plaza in a tranquil scene dominated by Machu Picchu Mountain.
Above: A regal profile with long eyelashes.

Left: A baby llama running after its mother.
Above: Late afternoon at Machu Picchu.

GOLD

Exquisite objects were created for the Inca by talented artisans using gold from the mines in Peru. Not only jewelry, but masks, goblets, breastplates, life-sized llamas, and corn stalks were crafted. The gold bedazzled the conquistadors. They melted the items down and shipped the gold to Spain. Certainly the royal retreat of Machu Picchu would also have been embellished with gold objects, yet none were found by Hiram Bingham. When the Inca Atahualpa was captured by the Spanish, they demanded gold to ransom his life. Gold was collected from throughout the empire, and Machu Picchu would have been no exception. Unfortunately, the conquistadors killed him anyway. However, one object at Machu Picchu remained undetected because it was buried.

While taking soil samples for analysis near the tree in this small plaza, a rough wall was unearthed. Excavating to a depth of six feet, a bracelet was found propped between two stones next to the wall—perhaps as an offering to Pacha Mama, *Earth Goddess.*

Top: A reenactment of an Inca priest, who is wearing gold bracelet reproductions. Above: The gold bracelet has small holes to secure it to the wrist.

PHOTO CREDITS

In October 2007 Ruth and her husband Ken were invited to the Palacio Torre Tagle in Lima, Peru, where they were honored with the award of the Order of Merit for Distinguished Service to the Republic of Peru. The resolutions and medals were awarded by President Alan Garcia Perez for their many years of research and publications on the technological achievements of the Inca. The presentation was made by Foreign Minister Jose A. Garcia Belaunde, who stressed the contribution the Wrights have made in understanding and increasing the awareness of the historical and cultural legacy of Peru.

Published by Johnson Books, a Big Earth Publishing company.
3005 Center Green Drive, Suite 225, Boulder, Colorado 80301.
1-800-258-5830
E-mail: books@bigearthpublishing.com
www.bigearthpublishing.com

Cover and text design by Rebecca Finkel

9 8 7 6 5 4 3 2 1

Library of Congress Cataloging-in-Publication Data
Wright, Ruth M.
  Machu picchu revealed / Ruth M. Wright.
    p. cm.
  ISBN 978-1-55566-424-4
  1. Machu Picchu Site (Peru)—Pictorial works. 2. Inca
architecture—Pictorial works. 3. Incas—Antiquities—Pictorial
works. 4. Peru—Antiquities—Pictorial works. I. Title.
  F3429.1.M3W76 2008
  985'.37—dc22
                        2008028561

Printed in China

Front & back overleaf: From *Machu Picchu, a Citadel of the
Incas,* by Hiram Bingham, National Geographic Society, Yale
University Press, 1930.

Front end sheet courtesy *National Geographic* magazine.

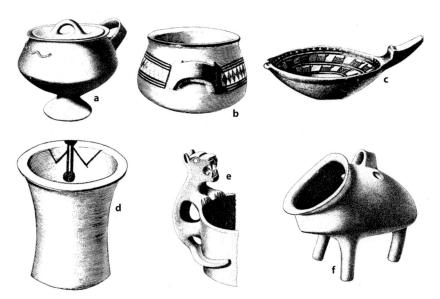

Household and ceremonial pottery found at Machu Picchu: (a) cooking pot;
(b) two-handled dish; (c) drinking ladle with bird's-head handle; (d) kero, *or cup;*
(e) handle in form of jaguar; (f) brazier.

PERU

UPPER
AGRICULTURAL
SECTOR

TERRACE
OF THE
CEREMONIAL
ROCK

GUARDHOUSE

INCA TRAIL FROM CUSCO

LOWER
AGRICULTURAL
SECTOR

MAIN
GATE

DRY MOAT

INCA CANAL

TRAIL TO GUARDHOUSE

UNFINISHED CANAL

INCA TRAIL TO
DRAWBRIDGE

INCA TRAIL
MACHU PICCHU
MOUNTAIN

INCA TRAIL
TO INTIPUNKU
WINAYWAYNA
AND CUSCO

PERIMETER
WALL

TRAIL TO GUARDHOUSE

INCA CANAL

TO
TOURIST HOTEL

INCA SPRING

50